The Mermaids and the Dolphin

Bella
Twink
Jo
Henry
Anna
Spark

Written by Celia Warren
Illustrated by Jessica Secheret

Bella and Anna were deep under the sea. They were playing with their pets.

"Look, it's Jo!" said Anna. Jo was with Henry, her pet crab. He was shy.

"Our pets can do tricks," said Anna.
"What can Henry do?"

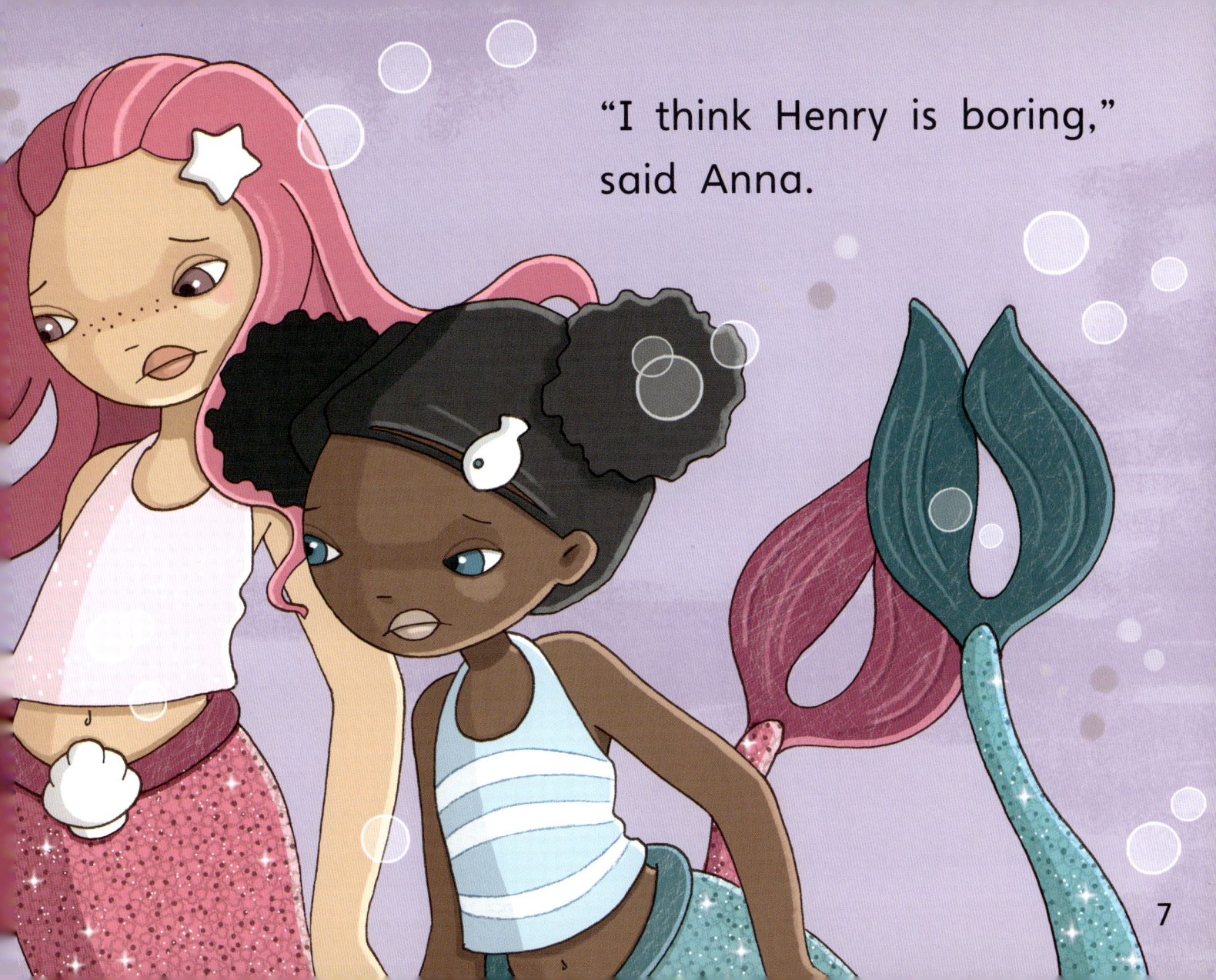

"I think Henry is boring," said Anna.

Just then, there was a noise.
"What was that?" asked Jo.

"Let's go and see," said Bella.

The mermaids saw a dolphin.

"He is stuck in the net," said Bella. "He needs help!"

Jo took Henry up to the dolphin.
Henry cut the net with his sharp claws.

The dolphin was free!
"Henry, you are a clever little crab," said Anna.

"Thank you, Henry," said the dolphin.
He gave the mermaids some stars.

Bella and Anna put their stars in their hair.

Jo put her star on top of Henry's shell. "Henry, you **are** a star!" she said.